PICNIC ON THE MOON

PICNIC ON THE MOON

Poems by
Charles Coe

The Leapfrog Press
Wellfleet, Massachusetts

Picnic on the Moon ©1999 by Charles Coe.

ISBN 0-9654578-2-6

Library of Congress Cataloging-in-Publication Data
Coe, Charles, 1952-
    Picnic on the moon : poems / by Charles Coe.
        p.   cm.
        ISBN 0-9654578-2-6
        1. Afro-American men–Poetry.   I. Title.
PS3553.0338P53   1999
811'.54–dc21   98-32361
                                              CIP

Book design and typography by Erica L. Schultz.

Printed in the United States of America
10 9 8 7 6 5 4 3 2 1

Published by The Leapfrog Press
P.O. Box 1495, Wellfleet, MA 02667-1495, USA

Distributed in the United States by
Consortium Book Sales and Distribution
St. Paul, Minnesota 55114
(612) 221-9035 / (800) 283-3572

Contents

Part III: Snapshots

Acknowledgments

I'd like to thank Elizabeth McKim for her generous encouragement and support. Special thanks also to my fellow travelers in the Gang of Four writing group: Gail Berger, Sherri Frank and Susan Fleet. And finally, I'd like to dedicate this collection to my sister Carol, for whom the best is yet to come.

PICNIC ON THE MOON

In the
Rear View
Mirror

Part I:
In the Rear View Mirror

Bossman pulled me to the side of the road.
And he said, "Boy, where you goin'?"
And I said, "Bossman, I'm goin' where I'm bound."
Bossman frowned.
And he said, "Boy, where you come from?"
And I said, "Bossman, I come from where I've been."

Praying in the Dark

When I was a child, God ate fish
on Fridays—spoke Latin
with an Irish brogue.

On the day
of my First Communion photograph
our small, brown faces smiled
at the count of three
and a great white light
blotted out the world.
(That photograph sits in a box
on a shelf in my mother's closet.)

The nuns spoke often of the
power of prayer; I prayed for snowstorms
so I could stay home from school.
When my prayers were answered
I'd press my nose against the glass
to watch those fat flakes
dance in the night.

We prayed the day
President Kennedy was shot.
From the corner of my eye

I watched Sister Edna's hands
wrapped around her rosary
her long, trembling fingers
the color of fish
that live on the ocean floor.

There are words from ancient ceremonies
I can still recite.
There is the remembered whiff of incense
and the sharp, smoky smell
of candles extinguished after mass.
There is the dim and distant sound of bells...

The nuns told us
God doesn't make mistakes;
all suffering is for the greater good—to teach
or to cleanse.

I try to remember that now
when I watch the news
or hear cries in the night
of those about to slip
beneath the waves.

Blues for Mister Glasper

This is how Mr. Glasper
my next door neighbor
spent his Saturday afternoons
in Indianapolis, Indiana,
during the summer of 1967:

He'd unfold a card table covered
with yellow plaid contact paper
and set it up in the middle of his scrubby
back yard. On the table he'd place
a dinky little record player—the kind
that only handled 45s—and plug it into a long line
of skinny, patched-together extension cords
that snaked through the crabgrass
and draped over the back porch rail.

Then he'd pile on a load of records,
plant his long, skinny body in a lawn chair,
and drift away on the Delta blues,
on songs of love gone wrong and pockets
full of empty. He'd sit, legs crossed,
eyes closed, in a feathered golf hat,
nodding to the beat, while voices rubbed raw by cotton dust
and homemade whiskey floated through his yard.

I could have stuck my fuzzy head over the fence
and asked what he was listening to,
but I didn't have no time for the blues. Man,

the world was on the move! Reverend King
was pulling black people out of the mud.
Sidney Poitier was getting *rich*
making movies, and acting
like a man! Not like some
bug-eyed darky, flapping his arms
and yellin' about some ghost.

So I didn't want to hear no twangy-twang,
old-timey, nappy-headed, watermelon-chewing music
played by refugees from a minstrel show.
I wanted Sam Cooke and Marvin Gaye, smooth and sharp
and all dressed up for Saturday night.
I couldn't hear the echoes of the Delta
in those brothers' songs.

I didn't realize then that blue is a primary color.

On Working with Slate Roofing Shingles

Though their gray, bland faces seem
to reveal nothing
slate shingles will tell you
how they want to be handled.
They don't like being bent
or tossed around.

Try lifing a small pile of slate shingles
and you'll soon discover
there is no such thing
as a small pile
of slate shingles.
So take your time.
They will sit
patient as stones
awaiting your pleasure.

There was a summer
of backaches and swinging hammers
when I helped take down
a leaky old slate roof.

Of the hundreds of shingles we handled
someone noticed that one had

writing on the back.

Looking closely we saw
two names scratched in,
and below,
a date:
August 11, 1917.

The shingles we lowered to earth
with block and tackle
and heartfelt curses
those two men
a lifetime ago
had put up nail by nail.

Passing that shingle around
we grew quiet
as if noticing for the first time
the blue sky
the fine ache of young muscles
the coolness of sweat
drying in the summer breeze.

In the House of Echoes

When her brother Albert finally died,
my mother was relieved
the tubes and wires
that had kept him tied so painfully to Earth
could finally be disconnected.

He hadn't let his sisters visit him those last few months;
my mother called it "old-fashioned masculine pride,"
but toward the end, when he was beyond knowing
who sat beside his bed, his four sisters
took their turns in the quiet room,
holding a hand as gray and light as dried grass.

At Christmas time, a few weeks later,
my mother and her five remaining siblings
sat around a dinner table where nine children
once argued and laughed
and lobbied for their parents' attention.
In a house grown quiet with years they talked
about their mother—round-faced and gentle,
always filling the house with the smell of baked hams
and apple pies—and of their father, quiet and serious,

his ox-blood leather easy chair and rack of Meerschaum pipes
sitting undisturbed for the thirty-five years since he died.

They told stories about Albert, and his brothers
Charles and Lawrence,
also gone, and they sipped egg nog
and nibbled ham sandwiches.
Finally, when the conversation lagged,
someone started singing Christmas carols,
and echoes filled the dark old house.

In the silence that followed the last carol,
a silence neither pained nor awkward,
merely thoughtful,
as each sat with his or her own memories,
my mother whispered softly,
to no one in particular,
"Three down, six to go."

Elizabeth by the Sea

In the photograph you sent,
wrinkles spin fine lines around your eyes
(the slow march of years, or are you simply squinting
as the sun sings
its rainbowed death song—paints
your skin in hues of rose and gold?)

I remember when you didn't like
to have your picture taken;
you always seemed trapped.
Caged. (The forced, unconvincing smile,
your shoulders hunched,
like someone from a tribe who thought
cameras captured the soul.)

But in the picture I'm holding now,
your hands are at your side, relaxed,
your posture poised
and unafraid. No longer braced
for the unexpected blow.
Behind you, the sea,
frozen by the camera's eye,
rolls endlessly to shore.
Beneath the waves,
sharp-toothed beasts
that once would roam your nights
to feast upon your storm-filled dreams
now brood silently,
puzzled by your new-found strength.

For the Traveler, Far Away

Your suitcase lies silently
across the back seat of my car—
festooned with stickers that boast
of Paris, London, and Berlin—
its smug mouth shut tight
against my curiosity.

If it could speak
it might explain
how there can be
so much space
between two people
in one car—
acres, miles, galaxies
our small talk
struggles in vain to cross.

It seems so long ago
the night we met,
you in that black dress
that clung like a bad reputation,
me with backpack full
of crunchy granola
and unquestioned answers.
(Where are those answers now?
Stuffed like dried leaves
between the pages of books
I no longer read.)

So much I tried to say

the night before you left
but my weighted words
could not take flight
and later
as you lay in secret dreams
across the bed
I knew you'd already packed your mind
and gone away.

And though your body's
sitting next to mine,
you have not returned...

so I will drive you
to your mother's house—
face that brittle smile
and the glint of lamplight
on her crimson nails—
and then, I will watch you fly away
like the birds,
who seeking shelter
from a coming storm,
streak like darts
across the lowering sky.

The Weight of Words Unspoken
for Terri

It was
I admit
an act
of cowardice
to keep driving
after realizing
the crushed calico ball
I saw
lying by the side
of the road
on the way
to your house
was probably
your cat.

That evening
while sipping your Beaujolais
I expressed mild and innocent concern
when you wondered aloud

why she hadn't come home for supper.
(She always came home for supper.)

The next day
when you cried the news
into the phone
I could taste
the words of sympathy
rotting in my mouth.

I wish now
I had taken your hand
(you had such small hands)
led you to that quiet
tree-lined road

and later
felt your tears
against my chest.

Get On Up!

Can anybody else here say
that in the summer of 1967,
when they were fourteen years old,
their mama took them to a James Brown concert?

Did you walk alongside her
through the gates of
a minor-league ballpark
on a hot, cloudless Indiana night
when the moon shone like a spotlight
on the rough wooden stage?

Was anybody else here sittin' beside their mama
on those hard benches
When James's band, the Famous Flames,
came out to lay down
a red carpet of funk
and the announcer whipped that crowd
like a bowl of black cream
'til the Godfather of Soul finally skated onstage
like a waterbug,
tellin' everybody 'bout his brand-new bag?

If your mama yelled like everybody else,
then let it now be told!
Let everybody know how
she clapped her hands raw
as James flew back and forth across the stage,

with sweat and grease from his conked-up hair
pouring down the front of his ruffled shirt,
purple satin jacket ripped off and tossed aside.
Let everybody know how she stomped her feet
when he grabbed that mic like a dog grabs a bone,
fell to one knee,
and begged for "just one more chance,
baby, baby please,"

And then, when he finally rose, shaking and spent,
and someone tossed a robe over his sloping shoulders,
and helped him trudge offstage,
did your mama scream when he suddenly froze

in his tracks—as if struck by the Holy Ghost—pulled away
from his helper, tossed that robe aside,
and ran back into the spotlight?

And is there anybody else
whose mama popped out of her seat
like a piece of toast
when the band scratched out the opening licks
of "Say it Loud, I'm Black and I'm Proud"?
And did she scream herself hoarse shouting out the chorus,
while James, wearing a coast-to-coast grin,
held his mic aloft to gather in the music of the crowd?

Was your mama there? Then stand up and testify!
Get on up! And Shout it out!

One for the Old School

On my last visit home, I drove by the old high school.
The school is closed now—the windows boarded. I was
in a hurry so I didn't stop, but my Memory hopped
from the car and before I could object, dashed up
the cement walkway—stepping around the tufts
of crabgrass growing in the cracks—and paused
before the large wooden double doors
at the main entrance.

I had a plane to catch, and tapped the car horn impatiently.
My Memory glanced back and waved, and then passed through
the locked doors as if they were smoke.

I yelled that there was nothing to see
but dust and mice, but my Memory ignored me.
It crossed the foyer into the main hall,
pausing to give the bust of George Washington
an affectionate pat, and then leaned
against my old locker to watch the parade of souls:
Rhonda Golden, whom I lusted after
but never had the nerve to approach; Sam Hatten,
on whose stereo I first heard Jimi Hendrix
and the Allman Brothers; there were a thousand other familiar,
but nameless, faces.

While I sat impatiently at the curb, my Memory,
humming the school fight song, wandered the halls.
It dropped in on the pep rally we held
for the state champion boy's basketball team.
It wandered through the cafeteria kitchen

and peeked in the ovens and pots. It watched the flights
of a million spitballs and rubber bands.
And after what seemed like forever, it finally returned
to reclaim the passenger seat.

"How can you be so inconsiderate," I yelled.
"Don't you realize I have a plane to catch?" I was angry,
but not really about missing a plane. I was angry
that my Memory could still experience and enjoy
all those things that were forever lost to me. I was angry
that all the institutions of my youth, and many of the people
are gone, never to return. But as I ranted, my Memory
remained silent; I could tell from its expression
of patient understanding it knew the real reasons
for my anger—it sympathized—and for some reason
this annoyed me even more.

Nevertheless, I began to feel foolish, so I shut up
and concentrated on driving. But after awhile,
I heard the rustle of paper and glanced over
to see my Memory, sitting quietly, flipping through
the pages of my high school yearbook, looking at the rows
and rows of faces—their youthful dreams and joys
and sorrows forever frozen—faces that peered back
through the thin, but impenetrable, curtain of years.

My Sister Read to Me

Nestled in my sister's lap
while she read a picture book
or fairy tale
I would trace trails
across the pages
that carried me to
other worlds.

I don't know how or when
My sister's path
carried her away from
sun and sky
to some strage world
light never reaches

where needles and spoons
and burning candles
are the nodding faithful's
machinery of prayer.

For a long time
she never read at all
just lay abed
behind closed door
television glowing in the
darkened room.

But something has changed
Now she emerges from her cave,

like a bear in spring
hungry, a bit confused
wincing at the unaccustomed light
shielding eyes that discourage questions
yet reveal all.

Rise up,
Daughter of Cleopatra,
who challenged mighty Rome

Daughter of Sojourner Truth,
whose white-hot gaze pierced the heart

Daughter of Artemis, goddess of the hunt,
arrows flying straight and true.

Rise up,
Daughter of ancient women warriors.

My sister,
you read to me,
and opened doors
you could not
walk through yourself.

Meditations

Part II:
Meditations

*My father, who used to paint houses, once complained
to his father-in-law, my grandpa, about a spell of rainy weather
that kept holding up a job. Grandpa listened thoughtfully for a while
and then said, "You ought to do what they do in China
when they get too much rain."*

"And what's that?" asked Dad. Grandpa paused to relight his pipe.

"Well," he said finally though a cloud of smoke, "They let it rain."

If What You Say is So

If what you say is so
that the world's heart
is cracked and crumbling
I must make ready
for the coming round
of gray days.
I will stand before cracked mirrors
practicing dyspeptic scowls to flash at babies
when their mothers' backs are turned.
When children play outside my window
I will shout down curses
like those dry old men who hate life
because it reminds them of death.

Will you then be satisfied?
When my eyes are covered
with that thin, tough film
that lets light neither in
nor out?

We can sit together then
in a cozy little room
and wiggle our toes before the fire
and sip our tea
and laugh at the fools
who still believe
that a life can be saved
by one hand
reaching for another.

It is a Wind

You can't explain
why the face you arrange
so carefully each morning
has suddenly slipped
and tilted on its axis.

You can't explain
the unspoken call
that pulled you along
the busy streets
past store windows
that waved their treasures
before your unseeing eyes.

And now, standing at the edge
of an unfamiliar park
you stop short
gazing out across the green fields.

It is a wind
that brought you here.
A soft wind
filled with half-remembered smells
flowing like a mountain stream
gentle, full of promise.

If the burden of your flesh tires you
just sit for a moment

and let the cooling breeze
linger on your skin.

If you have brought dark secrets
to this place,
whisper them softly—let the wind
carry them away
like the bits of paper
dry leaves
that tumble and roll across the grass.

If you have been squeezed breathless
by the weight
of all your plans and promises
then take your rest here
among the young lovers
who gaze into each other's eyes
and toss the word "forever"
like coins into a wishing well.

Picture This

Picture this:
A path in the woods
early morning dew
on green grass,
and all the colors
that headed south for the winter
are back

A young dog runs by
a flash of black and white
tongue hanging out.
She's chasing a squirrel
and she doesn't catch it
but she doesn't care;
she's already forgotten it
and now she sees a pond
so she charges for the pond
while her owner screams,
"Oh no, don't run through the mud"
but she ignores him
cause she's a *dog*
and she doesn't *care*
about his car's upholstery;
so she runs into the pond
and now she's standing

in the the mud at the water's edge,
shaking herself dry,
drops of water glittering in the sun
her tongue hanging out
and she looks up at you
as if to say the very thing
you needed most to hear:
"Ain't it great to be alive?"

Something in the Air

On this sunny day in early spring
a fickle hand has pulled aside that
cold, gray curtain and given us
a peek at what's to come.

Mama Earth has grabbed a golden broom
to sweep away the piles of dirty snow
and I'm staggering down the street
like a sun-struck mole.

Been underground so long,
but I'm tryin' to work my way back up
and there's something in the air
I'm trying to grab—something crisp
and green like a baby leaf—but
I just can't find the handle.

Feel like I'm trying to bum change
from some guy who's glidin' by,
lookin' neither left nor right,
girlfriend wrapped around his wrist
like a Rolex watch.

I'm standing here like somebody's fool,
head empty as a paper cup.

But I know there's something in the air.

And it's so close. Can't you feel it?

Wait!
        Stop!
Look left! Look right!

Listen to your red blood sing
in rhythm with the sweep
of Mama Nature's broom,

all you children with Technicolor hair
and pierced noses
trying to look so tough and cool,

and all you pissed-off teenage mamas
stomping down the sidewalk,
draggin' your kids behind,

and all you crazy drivers
pushing two thousand pounds of
carbon monoxide and bad attitude,

why don't we all just slow it down,
on this first real day of spring,
and take a big breath of
something in the air
that's crisp and green
as a baby leaf?

Crossing Vineyard Harbor

Seagulls follow the ferry
gliding stiff-winged
close enough to touch
still as a child's mobile
in a room without breezes.

Seagulls always follow ships
and plunge into the wake
for garbage tossed behind
tracing patterns in the sky
no craft made by human hands
could ever equal
while I,
without wings or feathers,
lean against the rail
to watch them swoop and dive—
their bodies dyed the colors
of the setting sun.

Sisyphus

I know this rock
as once I knew
my lover's breast.

I know its every curve and fold
each jagged edge that cuts and tears
my bruised and bloody hands.

And every night
while lying on my rough bed
of ferns and leaves
I carry deep within these bones
full memory of its mute,
uncaring weight.

At the time my labors first began
I would curse a certain god
that shape shifter,
seducer of unsuspecting virgins,
dissolute vainglorious oaf,
wine-stained beard
festooned with chunks of mutton.

I would gaze
at herons circling overhead
or goats rutting in midday heat
and wonder if the exalted one

had taken on such a humble shape
so he might amuse himself
by observing my daily comedy
and would one day
reveal himself to me—perhaps a dog
with a laughing human head—but that day
never came; it appears
that he who put me here
having set me to my task
has now moved on
to other entertainments.

I now save my breath for breathing
having learned that curses
will not shorten by a single moment
all the days I pass
all the days I pass
all the days I pass

wrapped in this rock's embrace.

Surplus Populations

Once, you needed us.
Walking silently along the furrowed ground
you watched our dark, hunched shapes
blend with the earth.

When you heard our voices
drift across the fields
you told yourself our songs
were the songs of happy children.

But now
there is little left to plant
little left to carry.
We look into the bright
faces of your new machines and know
that we are no longer needed.

So
where will we go?
What will we do?

We gather, restless.
on hot city streets

the ancient spirits of
of our tribes
dance before us,
shake their dry rattles,
chant the old chants,

but we cannot hear them.

Invisible to us
in this strange new land
they seek familiar holy places
and finding none
can only wander endlessly
among towering temples
glass and steel.

Meditation on the Loss of Empire

There comes a day
when after years at the top
the old bull elk can't meet
the young bull's charge
and shambles off into the dark woods.

The upstart
bloody face raised to the sky
sings his victory song
never sees his own fate
mirrored in the old bull's eyes.

Somewhere
at this very moment
hands begin to shake
that never shook before
sweat covers
a newly wrinkled brow
and chills creep quietly
into some heart
that never before
knew fear or doubt.

The game never changes—
only the players.
Today the young bull
is master of the world
but his bones will be the toys
of some child
yet unborn.

Over the Hump

1. This morning,
    while you walked to work,
    the wind,
    for the first time, ever,
    was at your back.

2. At lunch
    you pondered your tomato,
    and that moment
    within the sun-warmed earth
    when a seed said
         yes.

Boston Common Haiku

luscious green carpet
    I will lie for just awhile...
one more meeting missed

April Snow Haiku

Forsythia bush,
    yellow blossoms glazed with white,
you look so surprised!

Winter Lake Haiku

Frozen lake, clear ice,
    are you safe to walk across?
Faint cracks whisper, "No."

Opening the Refrigerator Door

Opening the refrigerator door,
I peer inside—in search of a miracle:
three slices of mushroom pizza,
or some leftover beef lo mein?
But the empty shelves recite
that simple law of physics
the mind knows,
but the stomach forgets:

"Nothing can be taken from a refrigerator that
was not first placed inside it."

But what if someday, behind that door,
something's there that wasn't there before?
Some patient morsel,
sitting in that cold white light?
Would I accept the gift, open-faced
and trusting as a child,
or would I slowly back away,
remembering that when the apple comes,
the snake must follow?

News from the Front

I have nothing interesting, nothing amusing to relate.

The shower leaked. A plumber came. He was unsmiling
and wore a tattoo. He replaced old fixtures with new.
I shall never see the old ones again.

The telephone rang. No one was there.

There is nothing to say. A package arrived
in the mail. Inside the package was a letter
promising eternal salvation in exchange
for a small donation. There was also
a plastic statuette of the Virgin Mary,
which I have given a prominent place
on my bedroom dresser.

I await her instructions.

A paper bag, filled with sand, sits in the trunk
of my car. The sand is for traction in the snow.
There is no snow, yet the bag remains.

There is no news. I returned two library books.
The books were several days overdue,

but there was no fine. The librarian said
there was a "grace" period for overdue books
before a fine was collected.

Grace is that few minutes we are allotted
each morning before being charged for the entire day.

Nothing has happened. The vegetables at the supermarket
are wilted. Automatic sprinklers were installed recently
in hopes that shoppers would equate moisture
with freshness. Sometimes the sprinklers
actuate themselves while the shoppers
are leaning over to inspect the produce.
When this happens, the shoppers become wet
and curse the produce.

I have nothing to report. No one is taking a shower.
The telephone does not ring. No snow falls.
The Virgin gathers dust.

The vegetables are silent.

Yo, Poets!

Here's a list of never-nevers:

Never read a poem
in a room
with a television set
(even if the set is off).

Never try to soften
a hardened heart
with a poem slipped
under a door
or left on a desk
or stuck to the 'fridge
with a plastic banana magnet.

Never read a poem to someone
who has to take a serious piss
or is expecting
an Important Telephone Call.

Never write a poem
when you could be making love
or eating a dish
of strawberry ice cream.

But most important,
when committing an act of poetry,
never be a slave to rules.

Picnic on the Moon

Lacus Veris, Aristarcus, Mima Arideus...
those names roll so smoothly off the tongue.

The Moon sounds like the perfect picnic spot—
a great place to bask in the warm solar breeze
and take a break from the earthly roar and rumble.

Yesterday a bomb went off beside a school bus.
Some child's blood-stained notebook lay
across a seat—one day's journal entry
in some ancient, endless war.

Right now, someone is cleaning his gun
in preparation for the evening news. His eyes
are shooting stars, spinning off into darkness.

Mare Imbrium, Oceanus Procellarum, Gassendi Crater...

Let's catch the Lunar shuttle—
spread a blanket on the soft gray ash
share our homemade pickles
with the Man in the Moon
and see just how far
a champagne cork can fly
in the airless lunar sky.

Last night I watched my laundry orbit the dryer
and wondered which shirts had been sewn
by children locked inside some windowless room.

Serenitatis Basin, Mare Crisium, Mare Tranquillitatus...

Don't be sad when we climb into the shuttle
for the trip home.
For we each will carry back
a cool and quiet place within ourselves
and the next time
we wake to the sound of gunfire
we can gaze into the night sky
and remember when

we nibbled grapes at the crater's edge
and watched the children
kick up clouds of lunar dust, their faces
smeared red—not with blood—but ketchup
and raspberry jam
as they romped beneath a blue-green earth
that glittered like a fragile and precious jewel
across the trackless miles of space.

Snapshots

Part III:
Snapshots

*Our faces lie
beneath a film
of time and dust.*

For Rosa Parks

It might have been easier
to let the moment pass.

It might have been easier
to rise with a sigh
from the creaking seat
trudge past those
pale, uneventful faces
and take your customary place.

Afterwards,
before walking the rest
of the way home
you might have stood
for a silent moment
in the wash of exhaust
to watch that bus
lumber off into the twilight.

But something happened...

Maybe your aching feet
and the driver's tone of voice

together tipped some hidden scales,

and the slow anger
that had grown for years
was finally called to birth.

Later,
when asked to explain,
you simply said:

"I was tired."

She Knows

An old black lady walks slowly
up a hill in Suburbville
'bout to wash somebody's floor—make it
shine like a brand-new car.
Folks drive by without a glance
find no lessons in that wrinkled face
but there is much that she knows:

She knows her mirror is her truest friend
(although the news is sometimes hard to bear).

She knows loneliness grows
like a hothouse flower
in the heart's fertile soil.

She know it's a long way
to the top of that hill.

If I had a car
I'd give her a ride
let her catch her breath
before she rang that bell

let her catch her breath
before she grabbed that
big old bucket
and dragged it to the sink
steam flowing 'round her head
like the waters of the Mississippi.

Poem for a New Widow

Your husband always considered earrings frivolous
so he never let you wear them. Oh, I know
you don't like the word "let."
He never forbade—you wouldn't stand for
being forbidden—let's just say there were battles
you chose not to fight.

You knew he loved you, in his solid
unspectacular way, like a tree loves water,
but when he died a part of you
was born again, even in the midst of sadness, the part
that laughs at "knock-knock" jokes
or works barefoot in the garden
and squeezes mud between your toes.

Yesterday, you bought a lime-green teddy bear
without explanation or apology. Last night
in the quiet, empty house
you sat it on the bedroom dresser
next to your new earrings.

Do you know how a circus elephant is taught to stay put?
When it's young, the trainer ties one end of a rope
around its foot and the other to a sturdy tree, or a pole.
The elephant tugs and tugs, and finally gives up.
When it's grown, it always remembers that a rope

around its foot means "no escape," so it won't try to pull free
even if the other end of the rope lies loose in the dirt.

For years, you bore your husband's
solemn Yankee thrift
but now that rope
has fallen to the ground
and you are walking
in surprised and careful steps
toward who you once were
and are again becoming.

Gathering Strawberries for Ice Cream

Two young sisters
skinny bookends
with tousled hair
and dirt-smudged faces
move along the rows
of strawberry plants
bending low to find
beneath the leaves
those last sweet nuggets
that escaped less careful hands.

When their wicker baskets brim
with berries plump and bursting ripe
they pad into the country kitchen
leaving barefoot trails
across the polished floor
and with large, solemn eyes,
baskets raised to heaven,
offer up those berries—dark
and dear as blood.

The Alchemist

for Etheridge Knight

The Alchemist would sit before his fire
muttering and chuckling to himself
and sipping dark potions
that were forbidden to the children.

His scarred brown face
glowed crimson in the flames
and when he spoke
the words rolled slowly off his tongue
like great stones
that gathered speed as they tumbled
through the listener's mind.

Those who came to sit
brought pieces of their souls
to toss into the fire.
Sparks would fly
flames would crackle
like chicken bones

in a hungry dog's mouth
and smoky fingers
climbed the sky
to caress the distant moon.

The Alchemist bore wounds
from wars of many sorts
and a thousand years of suffering
softened his bones
but still he'd smile
rub his stubbly chin
and lean to whisper
his warm-breathed secret in your ear:

While demons prowl the dark
just beyond the fire's glow
the poet stirs
a pot of words
and changes lead to gold.

For a Russian Soldier

Old men are rare
on the streets of Moscow.
They walk slowly, solemnly,
the breasts of their shabby gray suits
heavy with war decorations.

On buses and trains
they are the first seated
even before pregnant women.

Look closely—
in their opaque eyes
you will see reflections
of that distant winter
bodies frozen in the snow
some felled by rifles and tanks
others by hunger and cold.

Look closely—

you will see death
walk among his new children
quiet as a snowflake,
stopping here to whisper welcome
bending there to softly touch
a crystal-covered cheek.

Now, these old warriors
share the crowded streets
with busloads of smiling tourists
and ears that once bled from
the roar of artillery
now patiently endure
the booming strains
of rock and roll.

On the #1 Bus

The very large man
who squeezed me against
the window of the #1 bus
at 7:15 on a Monday morning
turned to ask
if I wanted to see his pet rattlesnake.
"It's very friendly," he claimed.
"It only bit the mailman twice."
"Thanks anyway," I said,
"but I only look at snakes on Tuesdays and Thursdays."
This seemed to satisfy him.
A bit later he asked, "You know what would really
liven up this bus? If ten thousand
killer bees suddenly poured through the door
and swarmed up the center aisle."
"Hmmm," I replied. He did have a point.

At the end of the day
on the return ride
a young woman hopped up
to leave the bus
and her wallet
with keys dangling
fell to the seat.
I grabbed it and tapped her on the shoulder.
"Excuse me miss, did you drop this?"
She looked wary for a moment
then her face opened like a flower.
I tucked her smile in my pocket
to warm the walk home.

Long Live the Queen

for Ella Fitzgerald

Fourth of July, 1958
at a backyard barbecue
my face buried in a plate of
hot dogs, baked beans and coleslaw,

when a voice sliced
through the grease and smoke—
a voice as hot as grandma's barbecue sauce
as cool as lemonade on ice—
a voice that changed everything.

A singer with a strong sense of rhythm
is said to "keep good time."
Ella, you didn't just keep time
You grabbed him by the ankles,
turned him upside down,
shook the change from his pockets
flipped him back onto his feet
slapped him on the ass

and sent him on his dazed
and dizzy way
cheek smeared with scarlet lipstick.

When you got it goin', eyes shut tight,
sweat rollin' down your face,
your sideman wore the same amazed expression
the apostles exchanged that time
Jesus called Lazarus back for an encore.

Five hundred years from now
on a mining ship light-years in space
some young jazz cat will be lying in bed
listening to you sing *Moonlight in Vermont*,
someone who's never breathed real air
or walked through a forest
but hearing your voice
will reach out
with eyes closed
to grab a handful of fallen maple leaves,
and breathe their faint perfume.

When Charlie Mingus Played His Bass

When Charlie Mingus played his bass
burnished wood glowed like black ice.

Eighth notes and sixteenth notes
dashed, naked,
through the smoke-filled room—
playing hide and seek—
and kissed each other
on the lips.

When Charlie Mingus played his bass
rivers danced with the moon—
left muddy footprints all along their banks.

Spirits of the trees recognized
their brother's song
and hummed along
deep in ancient forests where no light
ever shone—except at night.

You could hear
your heartbeat keeping time
and stray cats yowling at the moon
and dust motes floating in Pharaoh's tomb

when Charlie Mingus played his bass.

She Awakens

This poem was written to commemorate
the twentieth anniversary of Boston's Casa Myrna Vazquez,
a shelter for battered women and their families.

She awakens
late in the night

throws aside
the dream-soaked sheets
and sits upright in bed.

In this unfamiliar room,
the shadows are strangers
And night speaks a foreign tongue.

Her ears long for
the slow drip, drip, of her kitchen faucet
for the hum and click of the metal box

outside her bedroom window
that changed the traffic light
from red, to green, to yellow, to red
endlessly reciting its one unchanging prayer.

She rises
and steps into the darkened hallway.
In the home she left behind,
she could find the bathroom in the dark
while half asleep.

But now, she walks slowly
her careful feet search their way
across the creaking floorboards.

She fumbles
for the light switch
and squints
in the flickering fluorescent glow.
Her bruised face, framed in the mirror
reminds her where she is,
and why.

She remembers him
standing over her, yelling:

"You're lucky I put up with you
without me, you wouldn't be nothin'
nothin'
nothin'..."

She remembers
the squeal of tires
as he sped away.

She remembers rising from the floor
comforting her crying child
reaching for the packed suitcase
hidden beneath the bed
carefully unfolding the
well-worn piece of paper
with the telephone number
she had already memorized.

She remembers sitting in the cab,
as streets lights floated past.
She turned to look one last time

as the house grew smaller—
a distant receding shore.

She stares now into the bathroom mirror
her bare feet against cold tile
touches her face with shaking hands
as tears wash away the life she has left behind.

She could not tell you how
she broke the bonds of fear and pain.
She could not tell you why one seed opens
While another lies stillborn in the dark earth,
but she knows that a journey has begun
from which there is
no turning back.

She turns out the light.
It is easier now to find her way in this house.
The shadows have become her guides
and the room no longer unfamiliar;
entering, she hears the whispered
welcomes of those who have gone before.

She walks
softly to her sleeping daughter's bed

to watch the small
blanket-covered mound
rise and fall
in the full moon's light.

Her swollen lips
speak a silent vow:
"Never again."
Never again
will her daughter hear
the song of fist against face
that bitter melody
each generation
teaches the next.

And late in the night
in this quiet house
with one hand resting
on her sleeping daughter's brow

she awakens.

Possibility

The new snow covers everything.
This morning, the world was bathed
in that sharp-edged light
that comes in winter
after a storm blows through.
Outside my window, on the street below,
a small child, an electric-blue bundle
lets go of an adult's hand
to charge headfirst into a towering snowdrift.
When a snowplow comes
to shove aside the early morning quiet
the child stares, transfixed, as it rumbles past.

The new snow covers everything.
It covers cars that can be found only
by remembering where they were parked,
and digging like archeologists
seeking clues to some ancient civilization.
People who pass each other without speaking

each morning on the way to work
are now laughing and shoveling together,
good-natured butts of Mother Nature's joke.

The new snow covers everything.
It covers dogshit and cigarette butts.
It covers used condoms and losing lottery tickets
and under this impossibly blue sky
on what seems like the very first morning of the world
the city is an old whore in a white wedding dress
clutching, like a fistful of flowers,
the idea that in spite of everything
we know to be true
about the world and ourselves
we might, somehow,
begin again.

About the Author

Charles Coe is the winner of a 1996 Massachusetts Cultural Council Poetry Fellowship. A jazz and popular vocalist, he was born in Indianapolis, lives in Boston, and travels widely to perform and record his work.